The
Littlest
Christmas Tree

A Children's Christmas Play

Willard Rabert, Jr.

Wanda Reda

Lisa Sensinger

CSS Publishing Company, Inc., Lima, Ohio

THE LITTLEST CHRISTMAS TREE

ISBN 0-7880-1515-X   PRINTED IN U.S.A.

For
Amanda and Amber Schwartz
with thanks for their help

The Littlest Christmas Tree

Setting
The Woods

Cast
Twelve Trees
Angel
Family: Father
           Mother
           Elizabeth (Age 5)
           Matthew (Age 7)
           Sara (Age 10)

*(The trees should have their names on their person or should hold
a leaf, limb, bark, or pine cone to represent what tree they are.)*

Narrator: Deep in the forest there is a family of trees. The leaves
have fallen, and the ground and the trees are covered with snow. It
is December. As the trees shake off the snow, they talk about their
dreams for the next year, as they do at the end of each year. Each
tree has a special dream of what it wants to be.

Oak Tree: There is nothing more special than a church. I want to
be an altar where I can receive and give gifts to God and to people
in need.

Ebony Tree: Ha! That's too small a dream for me. I dream of
being a king's chair. Can there be anything greater than having a
palace for a home?

Maple Tree: I hope to be a sailing ship. I'll get to see places I've always dreamed about. Do any of you dream at night of seeing the world like me?

Ponderosa Pine: I've dreamed of sailing the open seas. I'll be the mast to hold the sails in your ship. Together we'll go to beautiful places the others can only imagine.

Apple Tree: You think only of yourselves. I wish I could have fruit all year, not just in the summer. That way I could share my gifts of apples with everyone all the time.

Cedar Tree: I agree with you, Apple. I've always dreamed of being a house to give shelter and warmth to a loving family. Is there any other tree that would like to be in my house?

White Pine: I would like to be in your house. I've dreamed of being a rocking chair, where a mother could sing songs to her children. When a mother rocks her baby, I feel love.

Cherry Tree: Can I be in your house, Cedar? I want to be a table, the center where a family gathers to eat and share laughter and joy.

Hemlock Tree: I love children. It's been my dream to be a part of children's happiness. It would make me happy to be a toy box to hold all their treasures inside.

Birch Tree: There's nothing like being held in a child's little hands. I would love to be a wooden doll or soldier so a little girl or boy would hold me, play with me, and love me.

Apple Tree: Old Tree, you're quiet. What do you dream?

Old Tree: I don't have fancy dreams like all of you. My dream is simple and real. I want to be the wisest of all the trees. Who else would protect the forest? The birds? The squirrels? The deer? Someone has to watch over all of us.

Narrator: As the trees continue to talk and argue over their dreams, off to one side stood a little Douglas Fir whose voice wasn't heard.

Douglas Fir Tree: (*Moping or sniffling.*) Why doesn't anyone listen to me? Don't any of you care about my dream? Just because I'm small doesn't mean I can't have a dream.

Ebony Tree: What king would have any use for a small tree like you?

Maple Tree: You're too small even to be a rowboat.

Fir Tree: (*Starts to cry.*)

White Pine: Don't listen to them, little Fir. Everyone is special, even you.

Old Tree: When you are as old and as wise as I am, you will learn that no matter how hard or how soft, how big or how small, every tree has a right to be needed and loved.

Fir Tree: All of you just wait. Every tree has the right to have a dream come true, to be anything he or she wants to be.

Narrator: The little Fir Tree seemed to get taller, and even his needles seemed more green and bright.

Carol: "Thou Didst Leave Thy Throne" (v. 3)

Narrator: The trees grew silent as they heard a family coming deep into the forest. (*Family enters from offstage.*)

Father: So many trees. Which one shall we pick for a Christmas tree?

Elizabeth: Where is the tree with lights on it?

7

Sara: Silly, the tree Daddy will cut down doesn't have lights on it. We put the lights on it on Christmas Eve.

Matthew: I want the biggest tree in the forest. How about this one? (*Points to Old Tree.*)

Sara: I want this tree. (*Points to Ebony Tree.*)

Mother: That looks like a very old tree. Old trees belong in the forest. That one is too hard to cut down. (*Pointing to Ebony Tree.*) Both trees are too big for our house.

Elizabeth: (*Goes to Douglas Fir Tree.*) This tree looks sad and lonely. It needs a family and love.

Matthew: That tree is too little. Elizabeth, trees don't have feelings.

Father: We don't know. Everything that God created has feelings, Matthew. That tree would look perfect by our fireplace. It would be so beautiful and special when we decorate it.

Sara and Matthew: (*Together.*) If we don't have any other choice, I guess it will have to do.

Matthew: But I would still like that one. (*Points to Old Tree.*)

Father: Now that we have all agreed, I'll cut down this tree. (*With cardboard ax, begins to cut at Fir Tree.*)

Carol: "Away in the Manger" (v. 1)

Narrator: The scene shifts to a starry night on the back porch of the family's home. The little Fir Tree is all alone, scared and cold. He (she) talks to the stars.

Fir Tree: I never got to tell the other trees my dream. Those people took me away and left me out here in the cold for days. All I ever dreamed about was being loved, not left all alone.

(*Angel appears on stage.*)

Angel: Little tree, don't give up hope. When you feel sad and unloved, look up to the stars and remember your dream. Dreams can come true. Even children are told to wish upon a star. You must believe.

(*Angel leaves.*)

Carol: "It Came Upon The Midnight Clear" (v. 1)

Narrator: It is Christmas Eve. The mother and father come out on the porch. Taking the little tree by the hand, they take the tree into the family room by a fireplace where the children are anxiously waiting. They have decorations in their hands.

Carol: "O Christmas Tree" (v. 1)
(*Carol sung by choir or all the trees of the forest while the tree is decorated.*)

Elizabeth: Look, Mommy and Daddy, the tree looks happy now.

Matthew: How do you know that? Did it tell you it's happy?

Mother: I don't know if it is happy, but it looks beautiful with the decorations.

Sara: It isn't just the decorations that make it look beautiful. It's pretty because it's loved.

Narrator: The little Fir Tree never knew the angel was right. His (her) dream came true. He (she) wanted to thank the angel if he (she) ever saw the angel again. He wondered if he (she) would.

9

Elizabeth: Mommy, don't all the Christmas trees have angels on top of them? Why don't we have an angel?

Father: Angels cost a lot of money. That's why we never had one on the top of our tree. One day we'll have a special angel for our tree.

Elizabeth: I'm going to bed and pray for an angel for our tree.

Mother: That's a good idea. Bedtime, everyone, and let's remember to ask in our prayers for an angel.

(*Family goes offstage and Tree is left alone.*)

Narrator: The little tree feels loved. The tree prays for an angel, not for himself (herself), but for the family who has made his (her) dream come true.

(*Angel comes on stage and goes beside Tree.*)

Fir Tree: You came back! I was hoping you would return. I wanted to thank you for helping to make my dream come true. The family who took me in is praying for an angel. I wish I could help them.

Angel: You can!

Fir Tree: I can?

Angel: Close your eyes and believe. (*Fir Tree closes eyes. The Angel goes behind Tree and holds up an angel over the tree's head.*)

Fir Tree: (*Opens eyes.*) Where did you go?

Angel: God has answered their prayers. Because you believed, Little Tree, I am their special Christmas tree angel.

Carol: "O Holy Night" (v. 1)

10

(*Elizabeth and Sara come running onstage near tree.*)

Elizabeth: We heard voices. Mommy, Daddy, Matthew, come look at our tree.

(*Mother, Father and Matthew come in near the two girls.*)

Elizabeth: Mommy, look! The angel. It is the most beautiful angel I ever saw.

Matthew: (*Rubbing eyes in disbelief.*) I don't believe it!

Sara: Where did it come from?

Father: When you dream and pray and hope hard enough, if you really believe, prayers can come true. We'll never know how the angel got here. Miracles happen for those who believe. Just as Mary and Joseph were blessed by the angel the first Christmas with the miracle of Jesus' birth, so we were blessed by God with our own, very special angel this Christmas.

Carol: "Joy To The World"